MW01533714

EASY FRIED RICE COOKBOOK

AN ASIAN COOKBOOK OF 50 DELICIOUS FRIED RICE RECIPES

By
BookSumo Press
Copyright © by Saxonberg Associates
All rights reserved

Published by
BookSumo Press, a DBA of Saxonberg Associates
http://www.booksumo.com/

ABOUT THE AUTHOR.

BookSumo Press is a publisher of unique, easy, and healthy cookbooks.

Our cookbooks span all topics and all subjects. If you want a deep dive into the possibilities of cooking with any type of ingredient. Then BookSumo Press is your go to place for robust yet simple and delicious cookbooks and recipes. Whether you are looking for great tasting pressure cooker recipes or authentic ethic and cultural food. BookSumo Press has a delicious and easy cookbook for you.

With simple ingredients, and even simpler step-by-step instructions BookSumo cookbooks get everyone in the kitchen chefing delicious meals.

BookSumo is an independent publisher of books operating in the beautiful Garden State (NJ) and our team of chefs and kitchen experts are here to teach, eat, and be merry!

INTRODUCTION

Welcome to *The Effortless Chef Series*! Thank you for taking the time to purchase this cookbook.

Come take a journey into the delights of easy cooking. The point of this cookbook and all BookSumo Press cookbooks is to exemplify the effortless nature of cooking simply.

In this book we focus on Fried Rice. You will find that even though the recipes are simple, the taste of the dishes are quite amazing.

So will you take an adventure in simple cooking? If the answer is yes please consult the table of contents to find the dishes you are most interested in.

Once you are ready, jump right in and start cooking.

— BookSumo Press

TABLE OF CONTENTS

ANY ISSUES? CONTACT US

If you find that something important to you is missing from this book please contact us at info@booksumo.com.

We will take your concerns into consideration when the 2nd edition of this book is published. And we will keep you updated!

— BookSumo Press

LEGAL NOTES

ALL RIGHTS RESERVED. NO PART OF THIS BOOK MAY BE REPRODUCED OR TRANSMITTED IN ANY FORM OR BY ANY MEANS. PHOTOCOPYING, POSTING ONLINE, AND / OR DIGITAL COPYING IS STRICTLY PROHIBITED UNLESS WRITTEN PERMISSION IS GRANTED BY THE BOOK'S PUBLISHING COMPANY. LIMITED USE OF THE BOOK'S TEXT IS PERMITTED FOR USE IN REVIEWS WRITTEN FOR THE PUBLIC.

COMMON ABBREVIATIONS

cup(s)	C.
tablespoon	tbsp
teaspoon	tsp
ounce	oz.
pound	lb

*All units used are standard American measurements

CHAPTER 1: EASY FRIED RICE RECIPES

CILANTRO AND BASIL FRIED RICE

Ingredients

- 4 tbsp vegetable oil
- 5 cloves garlic, finely chopped
- 2 green chilies, diced
- 2 C. cubed skinless, boneless chicken breast meat
- 2 C. cooked jasmine rice, chilled
- 1 tbsp white sugar
- 1 tbsp fish sauce
- 1 tbsp soy sauce
- 2 tsp chopped green onion
- 2 tbsp chopped fresh basil leaves
- 5 tbsp chopped fresh cilantro

Directions

- In a large skillet, heat the oil on medium-high heat and sauté the garlic till golden.
- stir in the chili pepper and chicken meat and stir fry till the chicken is done completely.
- Reduce the heat to medium.

- Stir in the rice, sugar, fish sauce and soy sauce and cook till well combined, stirring gently.
- Stir in the green onions, basil and cilantro and cook for about 1 minute.
- Serve hot.

Amount per serving (4 total)

Timing Information:

Preparation	15 m
Cooking	15 m
Total Time	30 m

Nutritional Information:

Calories	634 kcal
Fat	17.3 g
Carbohydrates	84.4g
Protein	32.8 g
Cholesterol	68 mg
Sodium	562 mg

* Percent Daily Values are based on a 2,000 calorie diet.

HAWAIIAN FRIED RICE

Ingredients

- 1 1/2 C. uncooked jasmine rice
- 3 C. water
- 2 tsp canola oil
- 1 (12 oz.) can fully cooked luncheon meat, cubed
- 1/2 C. sliced Chinese sweet pork sausage (lup cheong)
- 3 eggs, beaten
- 2 tbsp canola oil
- 1 (8 oz.) can pineapple chunks, drained
- 1/2 C. chopped green onion
- 3 tbsp oyster sauce
- 1/2 tsp garlic powder

Directions

- In a pan, add the rice and water on high heat and bring to a boil.
- Reduce heat to medium-low and simmer, covered for about 20-25 minutes.
- Remove from the heat and keep aside to cool completely.
- In a skillet, heat 2 tsp of the oil on medium heat and cook the luncheon meat and sausage till browned.

- Transfer the meat mixture into a bowl and keep aside.
- In the same skillet, cook the beaten eggs till scrambled.
- Remove from the heat and keep aside.
- In a large nonstick skillet, heat 2 tbsp of the oil on medium heat and cook the rice for about 2 minutes, tossing occasionally.
- Add the garlic powder and cook for about 1 minute.
- Stir in the meat mixture, scrambled eggs, pineapple and oyster sauce and cook for about 2-3 minutes.
- Stir in the green onions and serve.

Amount per serving (6 total)

Timing Information:

Preparation	10 m
Cooking	30 m
Total Time	1 h

Nutritional Information:

Calories	511 kcal
Fat	28.1 g
Carbohydrates	48g
Protein	17.1 g
Cholesterol	133 mg
Sodium	988 mg

* Percent Daily Values are based on a 2,000 calorie diet.

BACON AND GARLIC FRIED RICE

Ingredients

- 6 strips bacon, cut into 1/2 inch pieces
- 1 egg, beaten
- 8 green onions and tops, sliced
- 4 C. cold, cooked rice
- 1 tbsp minced garlic
- 3 tbsp Kikkoman Soy Sauce

Directions

- Heat a large skillet on medium heat and cook the bacon till crisp.
- Push the bacon to the side of the pan.
- Add the egg and cook till scrambled.
- Push the egg over.
- Add the green onions and sauté for about 1 minute.
- Stir in the rice, garlic and soy sauce and cook till heated completely, tossing continuously.

Amount per serving (6 total)

Timing Information:

Preparation	10 m
Cooking	30 m
Total Time	40 m

Nutritional Information:

Calories	213 kcal
Fat	5.1 g
Carbohydrates	31.8g
Protein	8.8 g
Cholesterol	41 mg
Sodium	692 mg

* Percent Daily Values are based on a 2,000 calorie diet.

Fried Rice Festival

Ingredients

- 1 1/3 C. uncooked white rice
- 1 2/3 C. water
- 3 eggs, lightly beaten
- 1/4 tsp salt
- 1/8 tsp ground black pepper
- 3 tsp vegetable oil, divided
- 1/4 lb. bacon, cut into strips
- 1/8 C. soy sauce
- 1 (10 oz.) package frozen green peas, thawed
- 2 green onions, chopped

Directions

- In a pan of the boiling water, stir in the rice.
- Reduce the heat and simmer, covered for about 20 minutes.
- Meanwhile, season the eggs with the salt and pepper.
- In small frying pan, heat 1 tsp of the oil and cook the eggs for about 3 minutes.
- Flip the eggs and cook for about 1 minute.
- Transfer the cooked eggs into a plate to cool.

- Then, cut the eggs into thin slices.
- Heat a large skillet on medium-high heat and cook the bacon till browned completely.
- Transfer the bacon onto a paper towel lined plate to drain and then crumble it.
- In the same skillet, heat the remaining 2 tsp of the oil with the bacon fat.
- Add the rice, breaking up the clumps and toss to coat with oil.
- Stir in the bacon, soy sauce, peas, eggs and green onions and cook for about 3 minutes.

Amount per serving (4 total)

Timing Information:

Preparation	10 m
Cooking	30 m
Total Time	40 m

Nutritional Information:

Calories	516 kcal
Fat	20.7 g
Carbohydrates	63.5g
Protein	17.3 g
Cholesterol	159 mg
Sodium	968 mg

* Percent Daily Values are based on a 2,000 calorie diet.

EASY JAPANESE GRILL FRIED RICE

Ingredients

- 1/4 C. olive oil
- 2 eggs, beaten
- 1 C. chopped grilled chicken
- 1/2 C. chopped green onion
- 2 tbsp chopped garlic
- 2 C. cooked white rice
- 3 tbsp soy sauce

Directions

- In a large non-stick skillet, heat the olive oil on medium-high heat and cook the eggs for about 2-3 minutes, stirring continuously.
- Stir in the chicken, green onion and garlic and cook for about 2 minutes.
- Stir in the rice and cook for about 2 minutes.
- Stir in the soy sauce and cook for about 3 minutes.

Amount per serving (6 total)

Timing Information:

Preparation	10 m
Cooking	10 m
Total Time	20 m

Nutritional Information:

Calories	226 kcal
Fat	12.6 g
Carbohydrates	17.1g
Protein	10.7 g
Cholesterol	80 mg
Sodium	491 mg

* Percent Daily Values are based on a 2,000 calorie diet.

WESTERN PACIFIC FRIED RICE

Ingredients

- 1 lb. bacon, chopped
- 4 cloves garlic, minced
- 6 green onions, chopped
- 2 carrots, sliced
- 1/2 lb. snow peas
- 4 C. cooked white rice
- 1/4 C. soy sauce

Directions

- Heat a large skillet on medium-high heat and cook the bacon till browned completely.
- Stir in the garlic, green onions and carrots and cook for about 2 minutes.
- Stir in the snow peas and cook for about 2 minutes.
- Stir in the cooked rice, 1 C. at a time, coating well with the grease.
- Cook till the rice is heated completely.
- Serve with a drizzling of the soy sauce.

Amount per serving (6 total)

Timing Information:

Preparation	30 m
Cooking	20 m
Total Time	50 m

Nutritional Information:

Calories	523 kcal
Fat	34.6 g
Carbohydrates	37.9g
Protein	14 g
Cholesterol	51 mg
Sodium	1253 mg

* Percent Daily Values are based on a 2,000 calorie diet.

Jade Garden House Fried Rice

Ingredients

- 1 1/2 C. uncooked white rice
- 3 tbsp sesame oil
- 1 small onion, chopped
- 1 clove garlic, chopped
- 1 C. small shrimp - peeled and deveined
- 1/2 C. diced ham
- 1 C. chopped cooked chicken breast
- 2 stalks celery, chopped
- 2 carrots - peeled and diced
- 1 green bell pepper, chopped
- 1/2 C. green peas
- 1 egg, beaten
- 1/4 C. soy sauce

Directions

- Cook the rice according to package's directions.
- Meanwhile in a large skillet. heat the sesame oil on medium-high heat and sauté the onion till golden.
- Add the garlic and sauté till lightly browned.

- Stir in the shrimp, ham and chicken and stir fry till the shrimp is pink.
- Reduce the heat to medium,
- Stir in the celery, carrot, green pepper and peas and stir fry till the vegetables become crisp-tender.
- Stir in the beaten egg and cook till just scrambled.
- Stir in the cooked rice and soy sauce and serve immediately.

Amount per serving (8 total)

Timing Information:

Preparation	10 m
Cooking	30 m
Total Time	40 m

Nutritional Information:

Calories	236 kcal
Fat	8.4 g
Carbohydrates	26.4g
Protein	13 g
Cholesterol	59 mg
Sodium	603 mg

* Percent Daily Values are based on a 2,000 calorie diet.

FRIED RICE CAULIFLOWER

Ingredients

- 2 C. frozen peas
- 1/2 C. water
- 1/4 C. sesame oil, divided
- 4 C. cubed pork loin
- 6 green onions, sliced
- 1 large carrot, cubed
- 2 cloves garlic, minced
- 20 oz. shredded cauliflower
- 6 tbsp soy sauce
- 2 eggs, beaten

Directions

- In a pan, add the peas and water and bring to a boil.
- Reduce the heat to medium-low and cook for about 5 minutes.
- Drain the peas completely.
- In a wok, heat 2 tbsp of the sesame oil on medium-high heat and sear the pork for about 7-10 minutes.
- Transfer the pork into a plate.

- In the same wok, heat the remaining 2 tbsp of the sesame oil and sauté the green onions, carrot and garlic for about 5 minutes.
- Stir in the cauliflower and cook for about 4-5 minutes.
- Stir in the pork, peas and and soy sauce and stir fry for about 3-5 minutes.
- Push the pork mixture to one side of the wok.
- Add the beaten eggs and cook for about 3-5 minutes, stirring continuously.
- Stir the cooked eggs into the pork mixture, breaking up any large chunks.
- Serve hot.

Amount per serving (6 total)

Timing Information:

Preparation	15 m
Cooking	30 m
Total Time	45 m

Nutritional Information:

Calories	366 kcal
Fat	19.2 g
Carbohydrates	15.8g
Protein	33.3 g
Cholesterol	132 mg
Sodium	1065 mg

* Percent Daily Values are based on a 2,000 calorie diet.

CHINESE BLACK MUSHROOM FRIED RICE

Ingredients

- 6 sticks dried bean curd
- 1 tbsp shredded black fungus
- 7 dried black mushrooms
- boiling water
- 3 1/4 C. water
- 2 C. basmati rice
- 1 tbsp butter or oil
- 4 eggs, beaten
- 3 tbsp vegetable oil
- 1 C. cubed carrots
- 1 C. chopped yellow onion
- 4 tbsp minced fresh ginger root
- 4 tbsp minced garlic
- 1/2 C. thinly sliced green onions
- 1 C. frozen peas
- 3 tbsp tamari
- 2 tbsp sesame oil
- fresh ground black pepper

Directions

- In a bowl of the boiling water, soak the the dried bean curd for about 20 minutes.
- In another bowl of the boiling water, soak the shredded black fungus and dried black mushrooms for about 20 minutes.
- In a pan, add 3 1/4 C. of the water and rice on high heat and bring to a boil.
- Reduce the heat to low and simmer, covered for about 5 minutes.
- Remove from the heat and keep aside, covered for about 20 minutes.
- In a non-stick skillet, melt the butter on medium-high heat and scramble the eggs till creamy.
- Transfer the eggs into a bowl and chop into bits.
- In another bowl, mix together the carrot, onion, garlic and ginger.
- In a third bowl, mix together the green onions and frozen peas.
- Now drain all the water from the bean curd, fungus and mushrooms.
- Remove the tough bits from the bean and cut the remaining into quarter-inch rings.
- Slice the mushrooms.
- In a fourth bowl, mix together the bean curd and mushrooms.

- In a wok, heat 3 tbsp of the vegetable oil on high heat and cook the carrot, onion, garlic and ginger till tender, stirring occasionally.
- Stir in the bean curd, shredded fungus and mushrooms and stir fry for about 1 minute.
- Stir in the spring onion, frozen peas and rice.
- Stir in the eggs, tamari, sesame oil and a few twists of fresh black pepper and remove from the heat.

Amount per serving (6 total)

Timing Information:

Preparation	30 m
Cooking	30 m
Total Time	1 h

Nutritional Information:

Calories	539 kcal
Fat	19.8 g
Carbohydrates	71.7g
Protein	19.9 g
Cholesterol	129 mg
Sodium	613 mg

* Percent Daily Values are based on a 2,000 calorie diet.

PEKING FRIED RICE

Ingredients

- 1 C. chopped Chinese roast duck meat, skin and fat separated and set aside
- 1/2 C. thinly sliced Chinese barbecued pork
- 6 green onions, thinly sliced
- 2 tbsp soy sauce
- 2 eggs, beaten
- 3 C. cooked long-grain rice
- salt and pepper, to taste

Directions

- In a large skillet, add the duck skin and fat on medium heat and cook for about 10 minutes.
- Increase the heat to medium-high and stir in the duck meat, pork, half of the green onions, and the soy sauce.
- Cook for about 5 minutes, stirring continuously.
- Add the rice and cook for about 5 minutes, tossing occasionally.
- Make a wide well in the middle of the rice, exposing the bottom of the pan.
- Add the beaten eggs in the well and cook till scrambled.

- Stir the scrambled eggs into the rice mixture and cook for about 5 minutes.
- Stir in the salt and pepper and serve.

Amount per serving (4 total)

Timing Information:

Preparation	15 m
Cooking	25 m
Total Time	40 m

Nutritional Information:

Calories	375 kcal
Fat	15.7 g
Carbohydrates	35.8g
Protein	20.7 g
Cholesterol	144 mg
Sodium	528 mg

* Percent Daily Values are based on a 2,000 calorie diet.

CURRIED APPLE AND RAISINS FRIED RICE

Ingredients

- 6 oz. shrimp - peeled, veined, and cut into 1-inch pieces
- 1 pinch salt and ground black pepper
- 1 tsp cornstarch
- 1 tbsp vegetable oil
- 1 tsp minced garlic
- 1 egg, beaten
- 1 C. diced button mushrooms
- 3/4 C. frozen mixed vegetables
- 1 apple - peeled, cored, and diced
- 2 tbsp raisins
- 1 tsp curry powder
- 1 tbsp light soy sauce
- 2 C. overnight steamed white rice
- 1 green onion, diced

Directions

- In a bowl, mix together the shrimp, salt, pepper and cornstarch.

- In a wok, heat the oil on medium heat and cook the shrimp mixture for about 5 minutes.
- Transfer the shrimp mixture into a plate.
- In the same wok, add the garlic and sauté for about 1 minute.
- Add he egg and cook for about 3 minutes, stirring continuously.
- Stir in the mushrooms and cook for about 5 minutes.
- Stir in the mixed vegetables and cook for about 3-5 minutes.
- Stir in the apple, raisins and curry powder and cook for about 3 minutes.
- Stir in the rice, soy sauce, salt and pepper and cook for about 3-5 minutes.
- Stir in the shrimp mixture and green onion and cook for about 2-4 minutes.

Amount per serving (4 total)

Timing Information:

Preparation	30 m
Cooking	25 m
Total Time	55 m

Nutritional Information:

Calories	248 kcal
Fat	5.6 g
Carbohydrates	37.5g
Protein	12.7 g
Cholesterol	110 mg
Sodium	371 mg

* Percent Daily Values are based on a 2,000 calorie diet.

JAPANESE FRIED RICE CAKES

Ingredients

- 2 (8.8 oz.) pouches UNCLE BEN'S(R) Ready Rice(R) Garden Vegetable
- 1 C. panko bread crumbs
- 4 tsp soy sauce
- 3/4 tsp sesame oil
- 2 eggs, lightly beaten

Directions

- Set your oven to 375 degrees F before doing anything else and line a baking sheet with the parchment paper.
- In a bowl, add the contents of Ready Rice pouches and break up any clumps.
- Add the panko bread crumbs, soy sauce, sesame oil and beaten eggs. and mix till well combined.
- Place a 3 1/2-inch biscuit cutter over the parchment paper.
- With a large ice cream scoop, place a level scoop of rice into the biscuit ring and gently, press to fill the space evenly.
- Gently remove the ring.

- Repeat with the remaining rice mixture.
- Cook in the oven for about 10-15 minutes.

Amount per serving (5 total)

Timing Information:

Preparation	10 m
Cooking	10 m
Total Time	20 m

Nutritional Information:

Calories	230 kcal
Fat	5.1 g
Carbohydrates	43.7g
Protein	7.8 g
Cholesterol	74 mg
Sodium	944 mg

* Percent Daily Values are based on a 2,000 calorie diet.

PALEO FRIED RICE

Ingredients

- 1 (16 oz.) package soft tofu, frozen until firm
- 1 C. vegan Worcestershire sauce
- 1/2 C. soy sauce, divided
- 1 tbsp oil, or as needed
- 1/4 C. chopped green onions
- 2 cloves garlic, chopped
- 1 yellow onion, diced
- 2 C. frozen mixed vegetables
- 3 C. cooked white rice
- 1 tsp mirin (Japanese rice wine)
- 1 tsp sesame oil
- salt and ground black pepper to taste
- 1 (14 oz.) can bean sprouts, drained

Directions

- Thaw the tofu for at least 2 hours.
- Squeeze between paper towels to drain completely and transfer into a bowl.
- Add the Worcestershire sauce and enough soy sauce to cover and marinate for at least 1 hour.

- Drain the tofu and discard the marinade.
- In a large skillet, heat the oil on high heat and sauté the green onions and garlic for about 45 seconds.
- Add the tofu and stir-fry for about 1-2 minutes.
- stir in the yellow onion and stir-fry for about 2-3 minutes.
- Add frozen vegetables and sauté for about 2-3 minutes.
- Stir in the rice, mirin, sesame oil, salt, pepper and enough soy sauce to cover the rice.
- Stir in the bean sprouts and stir fry for about 1-2 minutes.

Amount per serving (4 total)

Timing Information:

Preparation	15 m
Cooking	10 m
Total Time	3 h 25 m

Nutritional Information:

Calories	413 kcal
Fat	10.8 g
Carbohydrates	61.6g
Protein	18.1 g
Cholesterol	0 mg
Sodium	3221 mg

* Percent Daily Values are based on a 2,000 calorie diet.

Sweet Thai Chile Fried Rice

Ingredients

- 1/2 C. frozen corn, thawed
- 1/2 C. frozen peas, thawed
- 1/4 C. water, divided
- 3 eggs
- 1 tsp butter
- 3 slices bacon
- 2 tbsp peanut oil
- 4 C. cooked medium-grain jasmine rice, cold
- 3 tbsp sriracha sauce
- 2 tbsp soy sauce
- 2 tbsp fish sauce

Directions

- In a microwave safe bowl, mix together the corn, peas and 1 tbsp of the water and microwave on High for about 2 minutes.
- In a small bowl, add 1 tbsp of the water and 1 egg and beat well.
- In a large skillet, melt the butter on medium heat and cook the beaten egg mixture fir about 1 minute per side.

- Transfer cooked egg into to a plate and cut into slices.
- Repeat with remaining 2 tbsp of the water and remaining 2 eggs.
- Heat a large skillet on medium-high heat and cook for about 10 minutes, flipping occasionally.
- Transfer the bacon onto a paper towel lined plate to drain and then chop it.
- Swirl the same skillet with the oil and heat on high heat.
- With the wet fingers, beak up large clumps of the rice.
- Add 2 handfuls of rice into the skillet and cook for about 1 minute, stirring continuously.
- Transfer the rice into a bowl.
- Repeat with the remaining rice.
- Reduce the heat to medium and stir in the rice, sriracha sauce, soy sauce and fish sauce and cook for about 2 minutes.
- Add corn, peas, eggs and bacon and cook for about 3 minutes, tossing occasionally.

Amount per serving (4 total)

Timing Information:

Preparation	10 m
Cooking	26 m
Total Time	36 m

Nutritional Information:

Calories	446 kcal
Fat	14.9 g
Carbohydrates	62.4g
Protein	14.1 g
Cholesterol	150 mg
Sodium	1712 mg

* Percent Daily Values are based on a 2,000 calorie diet.

CAJUN FRIED RICE

Ingredients

- 2 C. water
- 1 C. white rice
- 1 tsp dried oregano
- 1 tsp dried basil
- 1/2 tsp dried sage
- 1/2 tsp cayenne pepper
- 1/2 tsp Creole seasoning
- 1/2 tsp salt
- 1/2 tsp ground black pepper
- 1/2 tsp lemon zest
- 3 tbsp extra-virgin olive oil
- 1 tbsp vegan margarine
- 1 green bell pepper, minced
- 1 carrot, minced
- 1 stalk celery, minced
- 1/2 small tomato, diced
- 1 tsp soy sauce
- 1 pinch salt and ground black pepper

Directions

- In a pan, mix together the water, rice, oregano, basil, sage, cayenne pepper, Creole seasoning, 1 tsp of the salt, 1 tsp of the pepper and lemon zest and bring to a boil.
- Reduce the heat to medium-low and simmer, covered for about 20-25 minutes.
- In a large pan, heat the olive oil and vegan margarine on medium-low heat.
- Add the rice and cook for about 5 minutes, stirring occasionally.

Amount per serving (2 total)

Timing Information:

Preparation	15 m
Cooking	30 m
Total Time	45 m

Nutritional Information:

Calories	612 kcal
Fat	26.9 g
Carbohydrates	83.1g
Protein	8.3 g
Cholesterol	0 mg
Sodium	1034 mg

* Percent Daily Values are based on a 2,000 calorie diet.

FRIED RICE IN THE MORNING

Ingredients

- 4 C. water
- 2 C. uncooked white rice
- 6 slices bacon
- 4 eggs, beaten
- 1 large yellow onion, chopped
- 1 C. frozen peas
- 4 green onions, chopped
- 1 1/2 tbsp soy sauce, divided

Directions

- In a pan, add the water and rice and bring to a boil.
- Reduce the heat to medium-low and simmer, covered for about 20-25 minutes.
- Heat a large skillet on medium-high heat and cook the bacon till browned completely.
- Transfer the bacon onto a paper towel lined plate to drain and then crumble it.
- In the same skillet, add the eggs in the bacon crease on medium heat and cook for about 13 minutes.

- Stir in the yellow onion, peas, green onion, and 1 1/2 tsp of the soy sauce and cook for about 5 minutes.
- Reduce the heat to low and stir in the rice, crumbled bacon and remaining soy sauce.
- Cook for about 1-3 minutes.

Amount per serving (6 total)

Timing Information:

Preparation	10 m
Cooking	40 m
Total Time	50 m

Nutritional Information:

Calories	357 kcal
Fat	7.7 g
Carbohydrates	56.5g
Protein	14 g
Cholesterol	134 mg
Sodium	523 mg

* Percent Daily Values are based on a 2,000 calorie diet.

FRIED RICE FOR LUNCH

Ingredients

- 3 tbsp peanut oil, divided
- 1/2 onion, chopped
- 2 large eggs
- 1 C. diced fully cooked ham, optional
- 2 tbsp butter
- 3 C. cooked brown rice
- kosher salt and freshly ground black pepper to taste
- 1/2 C. shredded Cheddar cheese

Directions

- In a skillet, heat the 2 tbsp of the peanut oil on medium heat and sauté the onion for about 3 minutes.
- Crack the eggs and cook for about 1 1/2 minutes, stirring continuously.
- Stir in the ham and cook for about 1 minute.
- Stir in the butter and remaining 1 tbsp of the peanut oil and heat for about 10 seconds.
- Stir in the rice and cook for about 3-4 minutes, stirring continuously.
- Stir in the salt and pepper and remove from the heat.

- Serve with a topping of the Cheddar cheese.

Amount per serving (4 total)

Timing Information:

Preparation	5 m
Cooking	10 m
Total Time	15 m

Nutritional Information:

Calories	491 kcal
Fat	30.5 g
Carbohydrates	37.4g
Protein	16.7 g
Cholesterol	142 mg
Sodium	700 mg

* Percent Daily Values are based on a 2,000 calorie diet.

HOUSE FRIED RICE II

Ingredients

- 2 tsp canola oil
- 2 eggs
- 1/2 tsp water
- 2 tsp sesame oil, divided
- 1/2 onion, diced
- 1 clove garlic, minced
- 1/4 C. frozen peas and carrots, thawed and patted dry with paper towel
- 2 C. cold cooked jasmine rice
- 2 tsp light soy sauce
- 1 tsp fish sauce
- 1 tbsp sriracha sauce
- 1/2 tsp white sugar
- 1/2 tsp salt
- 1/2 tsp ground white pepper
- 1/2 tsp mono glutamate
- 1/4 C. chopped green onion, divided
- 1/4 C. chopped fresh cilantro
- 1 cucumber

Directions

In a bowl, add the eggs and water and beat till smooth.

In a large skillet, heat 2 tsp of the canola oil on high heat and cook the egg mixture for about 2-3 minutes, stirring continuously.

Transfer the cooked eggs into a plate.

In the same pan, heat 1 tsp of the sesame oil and enough canola oil that covers the surface of the skillet and sauté the onion and garlic in oil for about 1-2 minutes.

Stir in the peas and carrots and cook for about 1-2 minutes.

Add the cooked eggs and stir to combine.

Slowly, add the rice, breaking the clumps.

Cook for abut 2-3 minutes, stirring continuously.

Stir in the soy sauce, fish sauce, sriracha sauce, sugar, salt, 1/2 tsp of the white pepper and mono glutamate and cook for about 2-3 minutes.

Remove pan from the heat and gently toss in the green onion and cilantro.

With a vegetable shredder, peel the outside skin of the cucumber to create a ragged design on the outside.

Cut the cucumber into the slices diagonally and arrange in a circle around the serving platter.

Place the rice in the middle of the platter.

Serve with a topping of the additional green onion and a dash of white pepper.

Amount per serving (2 total)

Timing Information:

Preparation	15 m
Cooking	15 m
Total Time	30 m

Nutritional Information:

Calories	906 kcal
Fat	14.8 g
Carbohydrates	168.2g
Protein	21.9 g
Cholesterol	186 mg
Sodium	1598 mg

* Percent Daily Values are based on a 2,000 calorie diet.

THAI FRIED RICE

Ingredients

- 1 1/2 C. uncooked white rice
- 3 C. water
- 1 tbsp curry powder
- 2 tbsp Asian fish sauce
- 2 tbsp pineapple juice
- 1 tbsp vegetable oil
- 1 lb. boneless chicken meat, cubed
- 1 onion, sliced
- 1 (20 oz.) can pineapple chunks, drained

Directions

- In a pan, add the rice and water on high heat and bring to a boil.
- Reduce the heat to medium-low and simmer, covered for about 20-25 minutes.
- Remove from the heat and keep aside.
- In a small bowl, mix together the curry powder, fish sauce and pineapple juice.
- In a large skillet, heat the vegetable oil on medium-high heat and sear the chicken and onion for about 5 minutes.

- Stir in the cooked rice, pineapple chunks and curry mixture and cook for about 5-10 minutes.

Amount per serving (6 total)

Timing Information:

Preparation	15 m
Cooking	30 m
Total Time	45 m

Nutritional Information:

Calories	352 kcal
Fat	6.1 g
Carbohydrates	56.9g
Protein	17 g
Cholesterol	38 mg
Sodium	409 mg

* Percent Daily Values are based on a 2,000 calorie diet.

6-INGREDIENT FRIED RICE

Ingredients

- 1/4 C. vegetable oil
- 1/2 C. sliced Chinese sweet pork sausage (lup cheong)
- 1 large egg, beaten
- 1 1/2 tsp salt, divided
- 1/2 C. chopped bok choy
- 2 C. cold, cooked jasmine rice

Directions

- In a large skillet, heat the oil on medium-high heat and cook the sausage and egg for about 2 minutes.
- Stir in 1 tsp of the salt and bok choy and cook for about 2-3 minutes.
- Crumble the rice in the skillet and cook till warmed, breaking the clumps.

Amount per serving (1 total)

Timing Information:

Preparation	10 m
Cooking	15 m
Total Time	25 m

Nutritional Information:

Calories	2192 kcal
Fat	85.4 g
Carbohydrates	302.2g
Protein	50.2 g
Cholesterol	186 mg
Sodium	4303 mg

* Percent Daily Values are based on a 2,000 calorie diet.

FRIED RICE LUNCH BOX

Ingredients

- 2 tsp peanut oil
- 1 egg, beaten
- 1 tsp minced fresh ginger root
- 1 clove garlic, minced
- 3 tbsp reduced-teriyaki sauce
- 2 tbsp lime juice
- 1 tsp brown sugar
- 1/4 tsp salt
- 1/8 tsp red pepper flakes
- 3 C. cold cooked rice
- 2/3 C. frozen peas, thawed
- 2/3 C. frozen carrot slices, thawed
- 2/3 C. frozen chopped broccoli, thawed
- 1/4 C. sliced green onion (green part only)

Directions

- In a large skillet, heat the oil on medium-high heat and cook the egg for about 3-5 minutes, stirring continuously.
- Transfer egg into a plate.

- In the same skillet, add the ginger and garlic and sauté for about 1 minute.
- Stir in the teriyaki sauce, lime juice, brown sugar, salt and red pepper flakes and bring to a boil.
- Reduce the heat to medium and cook for about 2 minutes.
- Crumble the cold rice into the skillet and cook till warmed, breaking the clumps.
- Stir in the peas, carrots, broccoli and green onion and cook for about 7-10 minutes.
- Stir in the scrambled egg and cook for about 1-2 minutes.

Amount per serving (6 total)

Timing Information:

Preparation	15 m
Cooking	15 m
Total Time	30 m

Nutritional Information:

Calories	164 kcal
Fat	2.7 g
Carbohydrates	29.7g
Protein	5 g
Cholesterol	27 mg
Sodium	786 mg

* Percent Daily Values are based on a 2,000 calorie diet.

FILIPINO FRIED RICE

Ingredients

- 2 C. water
- 1 C. uncooked white rice
- 1 tsp butter
- 1 small onion, minced
- 1 large clove garlic, minced
- 1 tsp diced chile pepper
- 1 egg, beaten
- 2 tbsp soy sauce
- 1 tbsp sesame oil

Directions

- In a pan, add the rice and water and bring to a boil.
- Reduce the heat to medium-low and simmer, covered for about 20-25 minutes.
- In a large skillet, melt the butter on medium-high heat and sauté the onion, garlic and chile pepper for about 5-7 minutes.
- Stir in the cooked rice, egg, soy sauce and sesame oil and cook for about 3-5 minutes.

Amount per serving (4 total)

Timing Information:

Preparation	15 m
Cooking	30 m
Total Time	45 m

Nutritional Information:

Calories	239 kcal
Fat	6 g
Carbohydrates	39.8g
Protein	5.7 g
Cholesterol	49 mg
Sodium	482 mg

* Percent Daily Values are based on a 2,000 calorie diet.

Seafood Sampler Fried Rice

Ingredients

- 2/3 C. uncooked long grain white rice
- 1 1/3 C. water
- 3 tbsp vegetable oil
- 2 medium onions, cut into wedges
- 3 cloves garlic, chopped
- 1/2 tbsp white sugar
- 2 tsp salt
- 1 egg, beaten
- 1/4 lb. cooked crab meat
- 3 green onions, chopped
- 1 tbsp chopped cilantro
- 1/2 cucumber, sliced
- 1 lime, sliced

Directions

- In a pan, add the rice and water and bring to a boil.
- Reduce the heat and simmer, covered for about 20 minutes.
- In a wok, heat the oil on medium heat and sauté the onions and garlic till tender.

- Stir in the rice, sugar and salt and cook for about 5 minutes.
- Stir in the egg and increase the heat to high.
- Stir in the crab meat, green onions and cilantro and cook for about 2-5 minutes.
- Serve with a garnishing of the cucumber and lime slices.

Amount per serving (4 total)

Timing Information:

Preparation	15 m
Cooking	40 m
Total Time	55 m

Nutritional Information:

Calories	304 kcal
Fat	12.2 g
Carbohydrates	37.4g
Protein	11.6 g
Cholesterol	68 mg
Sodium	1294 mg

* Percent Daily Values are based on a 2,000 calorie diet.

TERIYAKI FRIED RICE

Ingredients

- 2 C. water
- 1 C. uncooked white rice
- 1 lb. lean ground beef
- 1/4 C. soy sauce, divided
- 3 tbsp teriyaki sauce, divided
- 2 tbsp curry powder, divided
- 1 (4.5 oz.) can sliced mushrooms, drained
- 1/2 C. frozen peas and carrots
- 1/2 tsp ground cumin

Directions

- In a pan, add the water and rice and bring to a boil.
- Reduce the heat to medium-low and simmer, covered for about 20-25 minutes.
- Heat a large skillet on medium-high heat and cook the beef with 1 dash of the soy sauce, 1 tbsp of the teriyaki sauce and 1 tbsp of the curry powder for about 5-7 minutes.
- Drain the grease from the skillet.

- Add the mushrooms and frozen vegetables and stir to combine.
- Reduce the heat to medium-low and cook for about 2 minutes.
- Fold in the rice.
- Stir in the remaining soy sauce, teriyaki sauce, curry powder and cumin and cook for about 5 minutes.

Amount per serving (4 total)

Timing Information:

Preparation	10 m
Cooking	35 m
Total Time	45 m

Nutritional Information:

Calories	435 kcal
Fat	14.8 g
Carbohydrates	45.9g
Protein	28.3 g
Cholesterol	74 mg
Sodium	1644 mg

* Percent Daily Values are based on a 2,000 calorie diet.

European Fried Rice

Ingredients

- 2 tbsp olive oil
- 1 large onion, diced
- 3 large carrots, shredded
- 1/4 head cabbage, shredded
- 4 cloves garlic, chopped
- 1 (16 oz.) package kielbasa sausage, cut into 1/2 inch dice
- 3 C. cooked white rice
- soy sauce to taste
- 3 eggs

Directions

- In a large skillet, heat the oil on medium-high heat and sauté the onions till soft and translucent.
- Stir in the carrots, cabbage and garlic and sauté till the garlic begins to brown.
- Stir in the kielbasa and cook for about 3 minutes.
- With your hands, break up clumps of the rice.
- Add the rice in the skillet and cook till heated completely, stirring continuously.
- Stir in the soy sauce.

- Slowly, add the beaten egg, one at a time into the rice mixture and stir to combine.
- Reduce the heat to medium-low and cook, covered for about 10 minutes, stirring occasionally.

Amount per serving (6 total)

Timing Information:

Preparation	30 m
Cooking	30 m
Total Time	1 h

Nutritional Information:

Calories	473 kcal
Fat	28 g
Carbohydrates	38.6g
Protein	16.3 g
Cholesterol	143 mg
Sodium	1055 mg

* Percent Daily Values are based on a 2,000 calorie diet.

FRIED RICE WITH SEOUL (KOREAN)

Ingredients

- 1 tbsp canola oil
- 1/4 C. ground beef
- 1 green onion, sliced, white and green parts separated
- 1 C. kimchi, drained and chopped
- 1 tbsp gochujang (Korean hot pepper paste)
- 3 C. cooked short-grain rice
- 1 tsp sesame oil
- 1 tsp butter
- 1 egg

Directions

- In a large skillet, heat the canola oil on medium heat and cook the ground beef and white parts of green onion for about 1-2 minutes.
- Stir in the kimchi and gochujang and cook for about 2-4 minutes.
- Add the rice and cook for about 3-5 minutes, stirring occasionally.

- Meanwhile in another skillet, melt 1 tsp of the butter on medium-high heat.
- Carefully, crack the egg into the skillet and cook for about 3-4 minutes.
- Stir in the sesame oil and top with the egg.
- Serve with a garnishing of the green parts of green onion.

Amount per serving (2 total)

Timing Information:

Preparation	15 m
Cooking	10 m
Total Time	25 m

Nutritional Information:

Calories	566 kcal
Fat	16.9 g
Carbohydrates	88.2g
Protein	13.5 g
Cholesterol	107 mg
Sodium	622 mg

* Percent Daily Values are based on a 2,000 calorie diet.

CHINESE FRIED RICE NO VEGETABLE

Ingredients

- 1 egg
- 1 tbsp water
- 1 tbsp butter
- 1 tbsp vegetable oil
- 1 onion, chopped
- 2 C. cooked white rice, cold
- 2 tbsp soy sauce
- 1 tsp ground black pepper
- 1 C. cooked, chopped chicken meat

Directions

- In a small bowl, add the egg and water and beat till well combined.
- In a large skillet, melt the butter on medium-low heat and cook the egg mixture for about 1-2 minutes, without stirring.
- Transfer the cooked egg into a pate and cut into thin slices.
- In the same skillet, heat the oil and sauté the onion till soft.

- Stir in the rice, soy sauce, pepper and chicken and stir fry for about 5 minutes.
- Stir in the egg and serve immediately.

Amount per serving (4 total)

Timing Information:

Preparation	5 m
Cooking	10 m
Total Time	15 m

Nutritional Information:

Calories	255 kcal
Fat	10.2 g
Carbohydrates	25.9g
Protein	14.1 g
Cholesterol	83 mg
Sodium	516 mg

* Percent Daily Values are based on a 2,000 calorie diet.

FILIPINO BREAKFAST

Ingredients

- 1 tbsp vegetable oil
- 2 C. shredded and chopped cooked corned beef
- 4 oz. spinach, chopped
- 3 eggs, lightly whisked
- 5 C. cooked rice
- 1 tsp garlic powder
- salt to taste

Directions

- In a large skillet, heat the oil on medium heat and cook the corned beef for about 3 minutes.
- Stir in the spinach and cook for about 2 minutes.
- Push beef and spinach to the sides of the skillet.
- Add the eggs in the center and cook for about 3 minutes, stirring continuously.
- Stir in the rice and cook for about 5 minutes.
- Stir in the garlic powder and salt and remove from the heat.

Amount per serving (8 total)

Timing Information:

Preparation	10 m
Cooking	15 m
Total Time	25 m

Nutritional Information:

Calories	295 kcal
Fat	13 g
Carbohydrates	28.9g
Protein	14.2 g
Cholesterol	117 mg
Sodium	602 mg

* Percent Daily Values are based on a 2,000 calorie diet.

TERIYAKI FRIED RICE II

Ingredients

- 1/2 lb. boneless skinless chicken breasts
- 2 tbsp vegetable oil
- 3 green onions and tops, chopped
- 1 carrot, julienned
- 1 egg, beaten
- 4 C. cold cooked rice
- 3 tbsp Kikkoman Roasted Garlic Teriyaki Marinade & Sauce

Directions

- Cut the chicken into thin strips.
- In a large skillet, heat the oil on high heat and stir fry the chicken, green onions and carrot for about 3 minutes.
- Add the egg and cook till firm, stirring gently.
- Stir in the rice and cook till heated completely.
- Stir in the roasted garlic teriyaki sauce and remove from the heat.
- Serve immediately.

Amount per serving (6 total)

Timing Information:

Preparation	10 m
Cooking	30 m
Total Time	50 m

Nutritional Information:

Calories	246 kcal
Fat	6.5 g
Carbohydrates	33.8g
Protein	12 g
Cholesterol	51 mg
Sodium	803 mg

* Percent Daily Values are based on a 2,000 calorie diet.

CILANTRO ORANGE AND PINEAPPLE FRIED RICE

Ingredients

- 1 tbsp vegetable oil, divided
- 2 eggs, beaten
- 1/2 lb. peeled and deveined medium shrimp
- 1 (1 inch) piece fresh ginger root, minced
- 2 red onions, sliced
- 3 green chile peppers, chopped
- 2/3 C. fresh pineapple, diced
- 1/2 C. orange segments
- 6 walnuts, chopped
- 2 C. cold, cooked white rice
- 1 tbsp soy sauce
- 2 tbsp chopped fresh cilantro
- salt and pepper to taste

Directions

- In a large skillet, heat 1 tsp of the vegetable oil on medium-high heat and sauté the onions till just tender.
- Increase the heat to high and heat another 1 tsp of the oil.

- Stir in the shrimp and cook for about 3 minutes.
- Transfer the shrimp into a bowl and keep aside.
- With the paper towels, wipe out the skillet.
- In the same skillet, heat the remaining 1 tsp of the oil on high heat and sauté the ginger for a few seconds.
- Stir in the onion and chile peppers and cook for about 1-2 minutes.
- Stir in the pineapple and oranges and gently cook till the fruit is heated completely.
- Stir in the rice, walnuts and soy sauce and cook for a few minutes.
- Stir in the egg, shrimp, cilantro, salt and pepper and cook till heated completely.

Amount per serving (2 total)

Timing Information:

Preparation	40 m
Cooking	20 m
Total Time	1 h

Nutritional Information:

Calories	591 kcal
Fat	17.5 g
Carbohydrates	76.1g
Protein	33.9 g
Cholesterol	359 mg
Sodium	732 mg

* Percent Daily Values are based on a 2,000 calorie diet.

FRIED RICE FOR THURSDAY NIGHTS

Ingredients

- 3 tbsp vegetable oil, divided
- 3 eggs, beaten
- 3 C. cold, cooked white rice
- 2 C. chopped cooked chicken
- 1/2 C. sliced celery
- 1/2 C. shredded carrot
- 1 C. frozen green peas, thawed
- 2 green onions, sliced
- 3 tbsp soy sauce

Directions

- In a large skillet, heat 1 tbsp of the oil on medium-high heat and cook the eggs till scrambled.
- Transfer the scrambled eggs into a plate and keep aside.
- In the same skillet, heat remaining 2 tbsp of the oil on high heat and stir in the rice.
- Add the chicken, celery, carrot, peas and green onions and stir to combine.
- Reduce the heat to medium and cook, covered for about 5 minutes.

- Stir in the scrambled eggs and soy sauce and cook till heated completely.

Amount per serving (6 total)

Timing Information:

Preparation	15 m
Cooking	20 m
Total Time	35 m

Nutritional Information:

Calories	315 kcal
Fat	13.1 g
Carbohydrates	28.1g
Protein	20.1 g
Cholesterol	128 mg
Sodium	559 mg

* Percent Daily Values are based on a 2,000 calorie diet.

YUKI'S SHRIMP FRIED RICE

Ingredients

- 2 tbsp olive oil
- 1 carrot, diced
- 1/2 green bell pepper, diced
- 2 C. shrimp, peeled and deveined
- 1/2 onion, diced
- 1/2 (15.25 oz.) can whole kernel corn, drained
- 2 cloves garlic, thinly sliced
- 1 tbsp olive oil
- 2 eggs, beaten
- 4 C. cooked rice, cooled
- 2 tbsp oyster sauce
- 2 tbsp soy sauce
- 1 tbsp butter
- 1/2 tsp salt
- 1 tsp butter
- 4 eggs, divided

Directions

- In a large skillet, heat 2 tbsp of the olive oil on medium heat and cook the carrot and green bell pepper for about 5 minutes.
- Stir in the shrimp, onion, corn and garlic and cook for about 5 minutes.
- Discard any liquid from the skillet.
- Reduce the heat to low and let mixture simmer.
- In another skillet, heat 1 tbsp of the olive oil on medium heat and cook 2 beaten eggs 2-3 minutes, stirring continuously.
- Add the oyster sauce, soy sauce, 1 tbsp of the butter and salt and toss to coat.
- In a small nonstick skillet, melt 1 tsp of the butter on medium heat.
- Carefully, break 1 of the remaining eggs in the skillet and cook, covered for about 3 minutes.
- Transfer the egg into a plate and keep aside.
- Repeat with the remaining 3 eggs.
- Transfer the rice into a serving plate and serve with a topping of the the fried eggs.

Amount per serving (4 total)

Timing Information:

Preparation	30 m
Cooking	30 m
Total Time	1 h

Nutritional Information:

Calories	553 kcal
Fat	22.8 g
Carbohydrates	61.2g
Protein	26.4 g
Cholesterol	375 mg
Sodium	1209 mg

* Percent Daily Values are based on a 2,000 calorie diet.

How to Make Fried Rice

Ingredients

- 1 lb. boneless chicken thighs, cut into 1/3-inch pieces across the grain
- 2 tbsp light soy sauce
- 2 tbsp brown sugar
- 1/4 tsp ground black pepper
- 2 tbsp vegetable oil
- 1/4 C. chopped onion
- 4 cloves garlic, chopped
- 2 eggs, beaten
- 3 tbsp light soy sauce
- 1 tsp white sugar
- 1 tsp ground white pepper
- 4 C. leftover cooked rice
- 1/4 C. thinly sliced green onions
- 1/4 C. chopped cilantro

Directions

- In a bowl, mix together the chicken thighs, 2 tbsp of the soy sauce, brown sugar and black pepper.
- Refrigerate, covered for about 2 hours to overnight.

- In a very large skillet, heat the vegetable oil on high heat.
- Reduce the heat to medium and sauté the onion and garlic for about 2 minutes.
- Increase the heat to high and cook the marinated chicken for about 4 minutes, stirring continuously.
- Push the chicken mixture to one side of the skillet.
- Place the eggs into the empty side and cook for about 2 minutes, stirring continuously.
- Stir in the chicken mixture, 3 tbsp of the soy sauce, sugar and white pepper and cook for about 1 minute.
- Stir in the rice and cook for about 4 minutes.
- Remove from heat and gently, stir in the green onion and cilantro.

Amount per serving (4 total)

Timing Information:

Preparation	25 m
Cooking	13 m
Total Time	2 h 38 m

Nutritional Information:

Calories	493 kcal
Fat	17.2 g
Carbohydrates	55.4g
Protein	27 g
Cholesterol	161 mg
Sodium	1214 mg

* Percent Daily Values are based on a 2,000 calorie diet.

FRIED RICE LUNCH BOX

Ingredients

- 1 C. uncooked jasmine rice
- 1/2 C. water
- 3 tbsp vegetable oil
- 2 cloves garlic, minced
- 2 tbsp chopped carrot
- 1 tbsp chopped onion
- 3 tbsp soy-based liquid seasoning
- 1/4 C. reduced-soy sauce
- 2 tbsp chopped green onion
- 1 tbsp chopped cashews
- 1 tsp raisins
- 1/4 tsp white sugar
- 1/4 tsp white pepper
- 5 canned lychees, drained and quartered

Directions

- In a pan, add the rice and water on high heat and bring to a boil.
- Reduce heat to medium-low and simmer, covered for about 20-25 minutes.

- Transfer the rice into a shallow dish and refrigerate till cold.
- In large skillet, heat the oil on medium-high heat and sauté the garlic for a few seconds.
- Add the carrots and onion and cooking till the onion begins to soften.
- Stir in the cold rice and cook till heated completely.
- Stir in the soy sauce, soy seasoning, green onions, cashews, raisins, salt and white pepper and cook till heated completely.
- Stir in the quartered lychees and serve.

Amount per serving (4 total)

Timing Information:

Preparation	15 m
Cooking	30 m
Total Time	1 h 45 m

Nutritional Information:

Calories	302 kcal
Fat	11.3 g
Carbohydrates	45.5g
Protein	4.7 g
Cholesterol	0 mg
Sodium	550 mg

* Percent Daily Values are based on a 2,000 calorie diet.

KOREAN CHICKEN CUTLETS AND FRIED RICE

Ingredients

- 2 skin-on, boneless chicken breasts
- salt and ground black pepper to taste
- 1/4 C. peanut oil, divided
- 1/4 C. Korean barbecue sauce
- 1 slice fully cooked luncheon meat, cubed
- 1 tbsp butter
- 1/2 C. chopped Napa cabbage kimchee
- 1/4 C. chopped pickled carrot and daikon radish
- 2 C. cooked white rice, cooled
- 1 tbsp soy-based liquid seasoning
- 2 tsp soy sauce
- 1 tbsp dried garlic flakes
- 2 tbsp gochujang (Korean hot pepper paste)
- 1 tbsp mayonnaise
- 1 tsp Sriracha hot sauce
- 1 green onion, chopped

Directions

- Place the chicken breasts onto a smooth surface and with a meat mallet, pound into an even thickness.
- Season with the salt and pepper and coat with 2 tbsp of the peanut oil evenly.
- Heat a heavy skillet on medium heat and cook the chicken for about 4 minutes per side.
- Coat the the top of the chicken with the barbecue sauce and cook, covered for about 1 minute per side.
- Transfer chicken into a plate and cover with a piece of the foil to keep warm.
- With a paper towel, wipe the skillet.
- In the same skillet, heat remaining 2 tbsp of the peanut oil on medium heat and cook the luncheon meat for about 3-5 minutes.
- In another skillet, melt the butter on medium heat and cook the pickled carrot, daikon, kimchee and rice for about 1-2 minutes.
- Stir in the liquid seasoning, soy sauce and garlic flakes and cook for about 3-5 minutes.
- Add the gochujang and luncheon meat into rice mixture and mix well.
- Cut the chicken into desired slices.
- In a small bowl, mix together the mayonnaise and Sriracha hot sauce.
- Divide the fried rice into serving plates and top with the chicken slices.

- Place the mayonnaise mixture over the chicken and serve with a garnishing of the green onion on top.

Amount per serving (2 total)

Timing Information:

Preparation	20 m
Cooking	18 m
Total Time	38 m

Nutritional Information:

Calories	824 kcal
Fat	47.4 g
Carbohydrates	64.6g
Protein	33.6 g
Cholesterol	97 mg
Sodium	1884 mg

* Percent Daily Values are based on a 2,000 calorie diet.

AMERICAN FRIED RICE

Ingredients

- 1 C. uncooked white rice
- 2 C. water
- 1/2 C. diced carrots
- 1/2 C. diced onion
- 4 tbsp butter or margarine, divided
- 4 eggs
- 2 tbsp milk
- 1 C. ketchup
- salt and pepper to taste

Directions

- In a small pan, add the rice and water and bring to a boil.
- Reduce the heat to low and simmer, covered for about 15-20 minutes.
- In a large skillet, melt 1 tbsp of the butter on medium heat and cook the carrots and onion for about 5 minutes, stirring occasionally.
- Add the cooked rice and stir to combine.
- Stir in the remaining butter and reduce the heat to medium-low.

- Stir in the ketchup and simmer for about 5 minutes.
- Remove from the heat.
- In a small bowl, add the eggs and milk and beat till well combined.
- Heat a nonstick skillet on medium heat and cook half of the egg mixture till firm, flipping once in the middle way.
- Transfer the cooked egg into a plate and cut in half.
- Repeat with the remaining egg mixture.
- Transfer the rice into a serving plate and serve with a topping of the egg halves.

Amount per serving (4 total)

Timing Information:

Preparation	10 m
Cooking	30 m
Total Time	40 m

Nutritional Information:

Calories	431 kcal
Fat	17.3 g
Carbohydrates	58.5g
Protein	11.8 g
Cholesterol	217 mg
Sodium	837 mg

* Percent Daily Values are based on a 2,000 calorie diet.

FRIED RICE GLITTER

Ingredients

- 3 C. cooked rice
- 2 tsp garlic powder
- 2 tsp onion powder
- salt and ground black pepper to taste
- 2 tbsp grapeseed oil
- 1/2 red bell pepper, chopped
- 1/2 carrot, chopped
- 1/2 stalk celery, chopped
- 1/4 C. water
- 1/2 C. French-fried onions

Directions

- In a large bowl, mix together the rice, garlic powder, onion powder, salt and black pepper.
- In a large skillet, heat the oil on medium heat and cook the red bell pepper, carrot and celery for about 5 minutes.
- Add the seasoned rice and water and cook for about 5 minutes.
- Add the French-fried onions and toss to coat.

Amount per serving (6 total)

Timing Information:

Preparation	15 m
Cooking	10 m
Total Time	25 m

Nutritional Information:

Calories	274 kcal
Fat	14.2 g
Carbohydrates	32.8g
Protein	2.5 g
Cholesterol	0 mg
Sodium	195 mg

* Percent Daily Values are based on a 2,000 calorie diet.

NEON FRIED RICE

Ingredients

- 3 eggs
- 1 tbsp water
- 1 tbsp butter
- 2 -3 tbsp oil
- 1 medium onion, finely chopped
- 3 garlic cloves, coarsely chopped
- 4 C. cold cooked white rice
- 4 tbsp soy sauce
- 1 tsp sesame oil
- 1/2 tsp fresh ground black pepper
- 2 green onions, finely chopped

Directions

- In a small bowl, add the eggs and water and beat well.
- In a large skillet, melt the butter on medium heat.
- Add the eggs mixture and cook for about 2 minutes, without stirring.
- Transfer the omelet into a plate and then chop it.
- In the same skillet, heat the oil and sauté the onion for about 2 minutes.

- Add the garlic and sauté for about 2 minutes.
- Stir in the cold rice, soy sauce, sesame oil and black pepper and stir fry for about 5 minutes.
- Stir in the egg and green onion and serve hot.

Servings Per Recipe: 6

Timing Information:

| Preparation | 15 mins |
| Total Time | 25 mins |

Nutritional Information:

Calories	277.8
Fat	9.8g
Cholesterol	98.0mg
Sodium	723.8mg
Carbohydrates	38.6g
Protein	7.6g

* Percent Daily Values are based on a 2,000 calorie diet.

HIBACHI FRIED RICE

Ingredients

- 4 C. cooked rice
- 1 C. frozen peas, thawed
- 2 tbsp carrots, finely diced
- 2 eggs, beaten
- 1/2 C. onion, diced
- 1 1/2 tbsp butter
- 2 tbsp soy sauce
- salt
- pepper

Directions

- In a pan, add 2 C. of the water and a pinch of the salt and bring to a boil.
- Stir in the rice and reduce the heat to low.
- Simmer, covered for about 20 minutes.
- Transfer the rice into a large bowl and refrigerate to cool.
- In a small pan, add the eggs on medium heat and cook till scrambled, breaking into small pieces.
- After cooling, remove the bowl of rice from the refrigerator.

- In the bowl of rice, add peas, grated carrot, scrambled egg and diced onion and gently, toss to coat.
- In a large frying pan, melt the butter on medium-high heat and cook the rice mixture with the soy sauce, a pinch of salt and pepper for about 6-8 minutes, stirring occasionally.

Servings Per Recipe: 4

Timing Information:

Preparation	0 mins
Total Time	40 mins

Nutritional Information:

Calories	356.5
Fat	7.2g1
Cholesterol	104.4mg
Sodium	616.0mg
Carbohydrates	60.6g
Protein	10.5g

* Percent Daily Values are based on a 2,000 calorie diet.

FRIED RICE IN JAKARTA

Ingredients

- 2 C. uncooked long-grain white rice
- 2 eggs, beaten
- 2 tsp sesame oil
- 1/2 tsp salt
- 8 oz. boneless skinless chicken thighs, cut into 1/2 inch strips
- 6 oz. raw shrimp, peeled
- 2 tbsp vegetable oil
- 2 tbsp chopped garlic
- 1 medium onion, finely chopped
- 2 tsp finely chopped fresh ginger root
- 1 tbsp dried shrimp paste
- 1/2 tsp fresh ground black pepper
- 1 tbsp chili bean sauce
- 1 tbsp oyster sauce
- 1 tbsp dark soy sauce

GARNISH

- 3 tbsp finely chopped spring onions
- 1/2 C. fresh cilantro leaves, chopped

Directions

- In a large pan of salted water, cook the rice till tender.
- Drain the rice and spread onto a baking sheet to cool for at least 2 hours.
- In a bowl, add the eggs, sesame oil and salt and beat till well combined.
- I a large frying pan, heat the oil till slightly smoking and stir fry the onions, ginger, shrimp paste, garlic and pepper for about 2 minutes, squashing the shrimp paste.
- Stir in the chicken and shrimp and stir fry for about 2 minutes.
- Stir in the rice and stir fry for about 3 minutes.
- Stir in the chili bean sauce, oyster sauce and soy sauce and stir fry for about 2 minutes.
- Stir in the egg mixture and stir fry for about 1 minute.
- Serve hot with a garnishing of the spring onion and fresh cilantro.

Servings Per Recipe: 6

Timing Information:

Preparation	15 mins
Total Time	25 mins

Nutritional Information:

Calories	382.9
Fat	9.8g
Cholesterol	129.2mg
Sodium	497.9mg2
Carbohydrates	53.1g
Protein	18.3g

* Percent Daily Values are based on a 2,000 calorie diet.

Hawaiian Fried Rice II

Ingredients

- 4 1/2 C. dry rice, cooked and cooled
- 6 -7 eggs, with a splash water, scrambled
- 1 (11 oz.) cans Spam lite, diced
- 1 yellow onion, diced
- 12 oz. frozen peas and carrots, thawed

SAUCE

- 1 C. aloha shoyu soy sauce
- 6 -7 tbsp for Kikkoman soy sauce
- 4 -5 garlic cloves, minced
- 2 tbsp oyster sauce
- 1 tsp sesame oil

Directions

- In a wok, heat 1/2 tbsp of the vegetable oil on medium-high heat and cook the eggs till scrambled.
- Transfer the scrambled eggs into a bowl.
- In the same wok, heat 1 tbsp of the oil on medium-high heat and sauté the onions and Spam till golden and starts to crisp.

- Meanwhile in a bowl, add all the sauce ingredients and stir till the sugar dissolves.
- Stir in the thawed peas, carrots and sauce mixture and bring to a boil on high heat.
- Cook till the mixture changes into a glaze.
- Slowly, add the cooled rice and eggs, breaking up any clumps of rice and cook till heated completely.
- Serve immediately.

Servings Per Recipe: 8

Timing Information:

| Preparation | 15 mins |
| Total Time | 40 mins |

Nutritional Information:

Calories	532.0
Fat	5.0g
Cholesterol	139.5mg
Sodium	2222.7mg
Carbohydrates	102.6g
Protein	17.5g

* Percent Daily Values are based on a 2,000 calorie diet.

AMERICAN MEDITERRANEAN FRIED RICE

Ingredients

- 1 C. rice, uncooked
- 1 -2 C. chicken stock
- 2 -3 slices bacon, cooked & chopped
- 2 tbsp shallots (green onions)
- 1 C. prawns, cooked
- 2 eggs
- 1 tbsp lemon juice
- 2 -3 tbsp soy sauce

Directions

- Grease a pan with a little olive oil and cook the eggs till set, breaking the yolks with the knife.
- Then, cut the eggs into small strips and transfer into a bowl.
- Add the rice and cook till browned.
- Add the stock and cook till all the moisture is absorbed.
- Add the shallots, egg, bacon pieces and cooked prawns and cook till heated completely.

- Stir in the lemon juice and soy sauce and remove from the heat.

Servings Per Recipe: 6

Timing Information:

Preparation	15 mins
Total Time	40 mins

Nutritional Information:

Calories	197.1
Fat	5.7g
Cholesterol	76.8mg
Sodium	479.3mg
Carbohydrates	28.4g
Protein	6.8g

* Percent Daily Values are based on a 2,000 calorie diet.

Ho Chi Minh City Fried Rice

Ingredients

- 3 C. steamed white rice
- 1 C. diced carrot
- 1 C. diced broccoli
- 1 C. diced Vietnamese sausage
- 1 C. diced Vietnamese dried pork roll
- 1 tsp vegetable oil
- 1 tbsp diced onion
- 2 tsp fish sauce
- 2 eggs
- 1 tbsp of chopped cilantro

Directions

- In a skillet, heat the vegetable oil on medium heat and sauté the onion for about1 minute.
- Stir in the carrot and cook for about 7 minutes.
- Stir in the broccoli and cook for about 2 minutes.
- Stir in the sausage, dried pork roll and 2 eggs and reduce the heat to low.
- Add fish sauce, steamed rice, a pinch of salt and pepper and stir to combine well.

- Stir in the cilantro and cook for about 5 minutes.
- Serve hot.

Servings Per Recipe: 4

Timing Information:

Preparation	25 mins
Total Time	40 mins

Nutritional Information:

Calories	762.6
Fat	20.7g
Cholesterol	125.9mg
Sodium	827.2mg
Carbohydrates	119.5g
Protein	20.5g

* Percent Daily Values are based on a 2,000 calorie diet.

LIME FRIED RICE WITH PRAWNS

Ingredients

- 2 eggs, lightly beaten
- 1 (450 g) bags shrimp, frozen, raw, thawed
- 1 tbsp sesame oil
- 2 spring onions, sliced
- 1 garlic clove, crushed
- 1/2 C. Thai sweet chili sauce, sweet
- 1 tbsp dark soy sauce
- 1 tbsp fish sauce
- lime juice
- 3 C. cooked rice
- 100 g snow peas, trimmed, thinly sliced

Directions

- Heat a lightly greased frying pan and cook the beaten eggs for about 1-2 minutes.
- Transfer the omelet onto a chopping board and keep aside to cool.
- Roll the omelet and cut into thin slices.
- With the paper towels, pat dry the prawns.

- In a deep frying pan, heat the sesame oil and cook the prawns till they turn pink.
- Transfer the prawns into a bowl.
- Cover with a piece of the foil to keep warm and keep aside.
- In the same pan, add the spring onions and garlic on medium heat and stir-fry for about 1 minute.
- Stir in the sweet chills sauce, soma sauce, fish sauce, lime juice, prawns, cooked rice and snow peas and toss to coat well.
- Stir fry till the rice and prawns are heated completely.
- Gently, stir in the omelet slices and serve.

Servings Per Recipe: 4

Timing Information:

Preparation	15 mins
Total Time	25 mins

Nutritional Information:

Calories	379.2
Fat	7.3g
Cholesterol	234.7mg
Sodium	1364.6mg
Carbohydrates	50.9g
Protein	23.7g

* Percent Daily Values are based on a 2,000 calorie diet.

KING FRIED RICE

Ingredients

- 4 C. jasmine rice, cooked and cooled
- 1 C. crabmeat, shredded
- 1/4 C. cooking oil
- 1/4 C. soy sauce
- 3 eggs, beaten
- 3 tbsp green onions, finely chopped
- 1 tbsp sesame oil
- 2 garlic cloves, finely chopped
- 2 tsp black pepper, ground
- 2 tsp sugar
- 1 tsp Thai fish sauce

Directions

- In a bowl, mix together the sugar, pepper, soy sauce and fish sauce.
- In a large frying pan, heat the oil on medium heat and lightly, sauté the garlic and green onion.
- Add the rice and mix till well combined.
- Add the egg and cook till done.

- Stir in the crab meat and cook till well combined, breaking up the clumps.
- Add the sauce mixture and mix well.
- Serve immediately.

Servings Per Recipe: 4

Timing Information:

Preparation	15 mins
Total Time	25 mins

Nutritional Information:

Calories	915.9
Fat	21.8g
Cholesterol	158.6mg
Sodium	1188.1mg
Carbohydrates	156.0g
Protein	19.5g

* Percent Daily Values are based on a 2,000 calorie diet.

SPICY JALAPENO FRIED RICE

Ingredients

- 1/4 C. low-soy sauce
- 1 tbsp hoisin sauce
- 1 tbsp rice vinegar
- 8 oz. ground pork, optional
- 4 small chinese sausages, thinly sliced, optional
- 2 tbsp canola oil
- 1/2 tsp sesame oil
- 1/3 C. green onion, sliced
- 1 tbsp fresh ginger, grated
- 3 -4 garlic cloves, minced
- 1 jalapeno, seeded and minced
- 4 C. cold cooked jasmine rice
- 1 egg, beaten
- 1/4 C. cilantro leaf
- 2 tsp sesame seeds
- 1/2 C. fresh pineapple, finely diced

Directions

- In a small bowl, add the soy sauce, hoisin sauce and vinegar and beat till well combined.

- Heat a large skillet on medium-high and sear the pork till browned completely.
- With a slotted spoon, transfer the pork into a bowl.
- In the same skillet, sear the Chinese sausages till browned.
- With a slotted spoon, transfer the sausage into a bowl.
- In the same skillet, heat both oils and sauté the onion, ginger, garlic and pepper till just starts to brown.
- Stir in the pork and sausages.
- Add the rice, breaking up any lumps with your hands.
- Stir-fry till the mixture is heated completely.
- Stir in the the vinegar mixture and stir-fry till almost absorbed.
- Push the rice to one side of the skillet.
- Add the egg and cook till scrambled.
- Stir in the cilantro, sesame seeds and pineapple and remove from the heat.

Servings Per Recipe: 6

Timing Information:

Preparation	1 hr
Total Time	1 hr

Nutritional Information:

Calories	502.5
Fat	32.4g
Cholesterol	106.3mg
Sodium	1178.1mg
Carbohydrates	29.6g
Protein	21.6g

* Percent Daily Values are based on a 2,000 calorie diet.

ARIZONA FRIED RICE

Ingredients

- 1 lb boneless skinless chicken breast, cubed
- 1 (10 oz.) packages frozen corn, thawed
- 1 small green pepper, chopped
- 1 small onion, shopped
- 2 tsp canola oil
- 1 C. chicken broth
- 1 C. salsa
- 1 tsp chili powder
- 1/4 tsp cayenne pepper
- 1 1/2 C. uncooked instant rice
- 1/2 shredded low-fat cheddar cheese

Directions

- In a large nonstick skillet, heat the oil and sauté the chicken, corn, green pepper and onion till the chicken becomes golden brown.
- Stir in the broth, salsa, chili powder and cayenne pepper and bring to a boil.
- Add the rice and stir to combine well.
- Cover the skillet and immediately, remove from the heat.

- Keep aside, covered for about 5 minutes.
- With a fork, fluff the rice and sprinkle with the cheddar cheese.
- Keep aside, covered for about 2-3 minutes.

Servings Per Recipe: 6

Timing Information:

Preparation	10 mins
Total Time	30 mins

Nutritional Information:

Calories	255.4
Fat	3.4g
Cholesterol	43.8mg
Sodium	444.3mg
Carbohydrates	34.2g
Protein	22.5g

* Percent Daily Values are based on a 2,000 calorie diet.

Asian Fusion Fried Rice

Ingredients

- 4 chicken drumsticks
- 2 tbsp fresh ginger, grated
- 2 tbsp soy sauce
- 2 large carrots, chopped
- 15 oz. cooked rice
- 8 oz. sugar snap peas
- 1/2 C. red pepper, chopped
- 4 eggs, beaten
- green onion, sliced for garnish
- soy sauce, for garnish
- toasted sesame oil (to garnish)

Directions

- In a large skillet, heat 1 tbsp of the oil on medium-high heat and sear the chicken with half of the ginger and soy sauce till browned from all the sides.
- Add 1/2 C. of the water and cook, covered for about 15 minutes.

- Meanwhile in a microwave safe bowl, add the carrots, remaining ginger and 2 tbsp of the water and microwave on High for about 4 minutes.
- Add the rice, peas, red pepper and microwave, covered for about 5 minutes, stirring twice.
- Remove the chicken and juices from the skillet and transfer into a bowl.
- With paper towels, wipe dry the skillet.
- In the same skillet, add the eggs and cook for about 3-4 minutes or till scrambled.
- Stir in the rice mixture and cook till heated completely.
- Serve ye chicken with the fried rice and serve with a topping of the green onions, soy sauce and sesame oil.

Servings Per Recipe: 4

Timing Information:

Preparation	10 mins
Total Time	35 mins

Nutritional Information:

Calories	371.8
Fat	11.8g
Cholesterol	270.6mg
Sodium	659.1mg
Carbohydrates	39.7g
Protein	25.3g

* Percent Daily Values are based on a 2,000 calorie diet.

GROUND BEEF FRIED RICE

Ingredients

- 3 tbsp vegetable oil, divided
- 3 eggs, beaten
- 3 C. cold, cooked white rice
- 2 C. chopped cooked ground beef
- 1/2 C. sliced mushrooms
- 1/2 C. shredded carrot
- 1 C. frozen green peas, thawed
- 2 green onions, sliced
- 3 tbsp soy sauce

Directions

- In a large skillet, heat 1 tbsp of the oil on medium-high heat and cook the eggs till scrambled.
- Transfer the scrambled eggs into a plate and keep aside.
- In the same skillet, heat remaining 2 tbsp of the oil on high heat and stir in the rice.
- Add the ground beef, mushrooms, carrot, peas and green onions and stir to combine.
- Reduce the heat to medium and cook, covered for about 5 minutes.

- Stir in the scrambled eggs and soy sauce and cook till heated completely.

Amount per serving (6 total)

Timing Information:

Preparation	10 m
Cooking	15 m
Total Time	40 m

Nutritional Information:

Calories	315 kcal
Fat	13.1
Carbohydrates	28.1g
Protein	20.1g
Cholesterol	128mg
Sodium	559 mg

* Percent Daily Values are based on a 2,000 calorie diet.

FRIED RICE WITH ALMONDS

Ingredients

- 4 C. cooked rice
- 1 C. frozen peas, thawed
- 2 tbsp almonds, finely diced
- 2 eggs, beaten
- 1/2 C. onion, diced
- 1 1/2 tbsp butter
- 2 tbsp soy sauce
- salt
- pepper

Directions

- In a pan, add 2 C. of the water and a pinch of the salt and bring to a boil.
- Stir in the rice and reduce the heat to low.
- Simmer, covered for about 20 minutes.
- Transfer the rice into a large bowl and refrigerate to cool.
- In a small pan, add the eggs on medium heat and cook till scrambled, breaking into small pieces.
- After cooling, remove the bowl of rice from the refrigerator.

- In the bowl of rice, add peas, almonds, scrambled egg and diced onion and gently, toss to coat.
- In a large frying pan, melt the butter on medium-high heat and cook the rice mixture with the soy sauce, a pinch of salt and pepper for about 6-8 minutes, stirring occasionally.

Servings Per Recipe: 4

Timing Information:

Preparation	0 mins
Total Time	40 mins

Nutritional Information:

Calories	356.5
Fat	7.2g1
Cholesterol	104.4mg
Sodium	616.0mg
Carbohydrates	60.6g
Protein	10.5g

* Percent Daily Values are based on a 2,000 calorie diet.

THANKS FOR READING! JOIN THE CLUB AND KEEP ON COOKING WITH 6 MORE COOKBOOKS....

http://bit.ly/1TdrStv

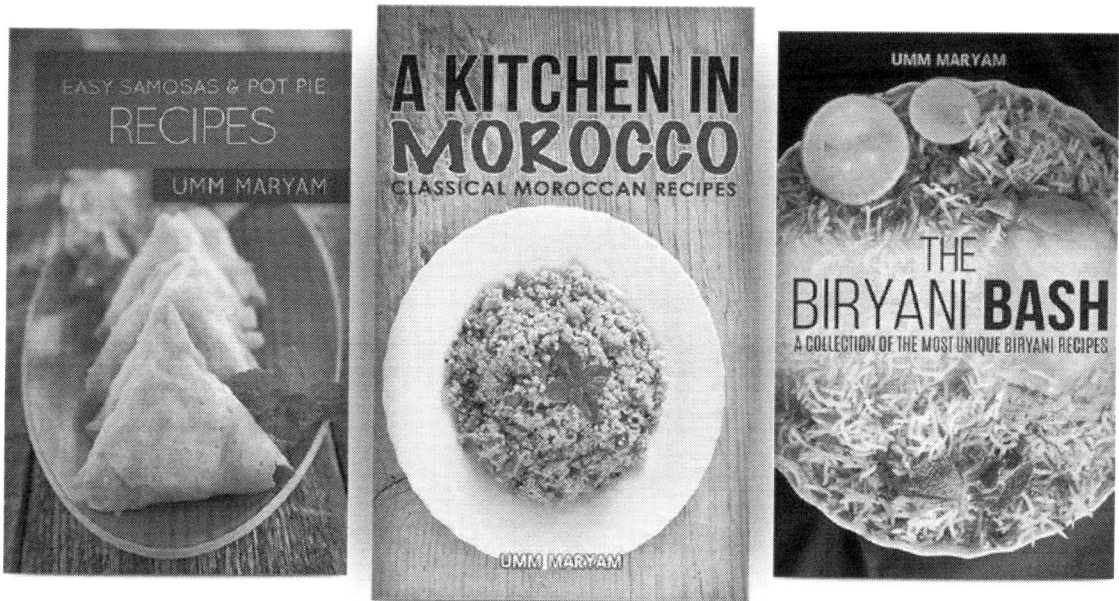

To grab the box sets simply follow the link mentioned above, or tap one of book covers.

This will take you to a page where you can simply enter your email address and a PDF version of the box sets will be emailed to you.

Hope you are ready for some serious cooking!

http://bit.ly/1TdrStv

COME ON...
LET'S BE FRIENDS :)

We adore our readers and love connecting with them socially.

Like BookSumo on Facebook and let's get social!

Facebook

And also check out the BookSumo Cooking Blog.

Food Lover Blog

27072923R00087

Made in the USA
Lexington, KY
27 December 2018